Notes

INSIDE A

PRAIRIE DOG'S HIDEAWAY

By Rex Ruby

BEARPORT
PUBLISHING

Minneapolis, Minnesota

Credits: Cover and title page, © Ralf Geithe/iStock, © 2009fotofriends/Shutterstock, © bmf-foto.de/ Shutterstock, and © Helen Davies/Alamy; Design elements throughout, © GlobalP/iStock, © Melinda Fawver/Shutterstock, and © Olhastock/Shutterstock; 4, © David Butler/iStock; 5, © AHPhotoswpg/ iStock; 7, © wrangel/iStock; 8–9, © Greg Vaughn/Alamy and © Arco / TUNS/Alamy; 11, © Ruby Tuesday Books Ltd.; 12–13, © Don Johnston_MA/Alamy; 15, © Roberto Dantoni/Alamy and © Andyworks/iStock; 17, © toos/iStock; 18–19, © HenkBentlage/iStock; 20–21, © Paul Bishop/Dreamstime; and 22, © Eric Isselée/Shutterstock.

Bearport Publishing Company Product Development Team

President: Jen Jenson; Director of Product Development: Spencer Brinker; Senior Editor: Allison Juda; Editor: Charly Haley; Associate Editor: Naomi Reich; Senior Designer: Colin O'Dea; Associate Designer: Elena Klinkner; Product Development Assistant: Anita Stasson

Library of Congress Cataloging-in-Publication Data

Names: Ruby, Rex, author.
Title: Inside a prairie dog's hideaway / Rex Ruby.
Description: Minneapolis, Minnesota : Bearport Publishing Company, [2023] |
    Series: Underground animal life | Includes bibliographical references
    and index.
Identifiers: LCCN 2022007034 (print) | LCCN 2022007035 (ebook) | ISBN
    9798885091404 (library binding) | ISBN 9798885091473 (paperback) | ISBN
    9798885091541 (ebook)
Subjects: LCSH: Prairie dogs--Behavior--Juvenile literature. | Animal
    burrowing--Juvenile literature.
Classification: LCC QL737.R68 R825 2023 (print) | LCC QL737.R68 (ebook) |
    DDC 599.36/7--dc23/eng/20220309
LC record available at https://lccn.loc.gov/2022007034
LC ebook record available at https://lccn.loc.gov/2022007035

For more information, write to Bearport Publishing, 5357 Penn Avenue South, Minneapolis, MN 55419. Printed in the United States of America.

Contents

A Busy Town

It's early morning in a little town. But instead of houses, there are small mounds of dirt. Suddenly, a prairie dog pops its head out of a hole in one of the mounds. The hole is the **entrance** to the little animal's **burrow**.

Prairie dogs dig their burrows on open, grassy lands called **prairies**.

Check Out a Prairie Dog

There are five different kinds of prairie dogs. But they all share a few things in common. Their little bodies have short legs, short tails, and small round ears all covered in brown or reddish fur. The largest prairie dogs can get to be about 17 inches (40 cm) long.

Black-tailed prairie dogs are the most common. They get this name from the color at the end of their tails.

A black-tailed
prairie dog

Prairie Dog Families

These furry creatures live together in small families. The groups usually have some adult **females**, their babies, and one adult **male**. Families can be part of larger communities called towns. Just as in a human town, each prairie dog family lives in its own small area, or **territory**. They dig burrows into their piece of land.

Hundreds of prairie dogs may live in a single town.

Inside a Burrow

All the adults in a family help build the burrow. Sharp prairie dog claws dig out several entrances. Below some, they make listening rooms. Then, they keep digging to make a long tunnel. The prairie dogs make a bedroom, where the family sleeps, and nesting rooms for when females are ready to have babies.

Prairie dogs make mounds of dirt around each entrance. This keeps rainwater out.

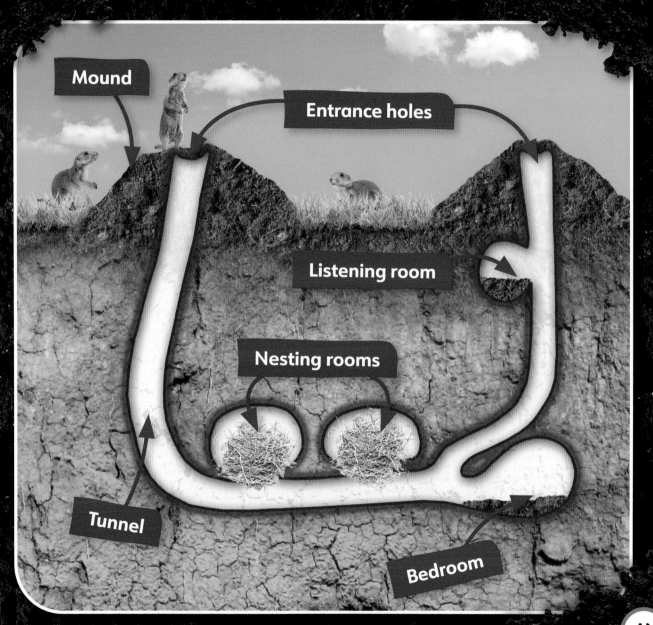

A Quick Escape

Why do prairie dogs dig listening rooms? They need to listen before they go outside. That's because these animals are in danger when they leave home. Many **predators** eat prairie dogs. If predators gets too close, prairie dogs dive underground to safety.

Prairie dog predators include coyotes, ferrets, snakes, and large birds.

A coyote might wait by a burrow for a meal.

Danger!

When aboveground, prairie dogs take turns watching for predators. If a prairie dog spots danger, it makes a sound. *Chirk, chirk!* When its family and neighbors hear this sound, they quickly dive into their burrows. Some prairie dogs use different sounds to **warn** about different kinds of predators!

Sometimes prairie dogs make loud noises with their feet to scare away snakes.

A Prairie Dog's Day

As the sun comes up, prairie dogs leave their burrows. They spend their days outside, eating grasses and small plants. If the weather is very hot, they may go back underground to cool off. On cold days, they return to the burrows to warm up, too.

Prairie dogs use their teeth to munch down tall grasses. Clearing away these grasses also helps them see predators coming.

Prairie Dog Babies

In spring, prairie dogs also come out to **mate**. Then, the female prairie dog uses dry grasses to make a nest in her burrow. Soon, she gives birth to a **litter** of babies. At first, the babies' eyes are closed and they cannot see. Their mother feeds them milk from her body.

A prairie dog mother usually has between three and eight babies in a litter.

Growing Up

After six weeks, baby prairie dogs can leave their burrows for the first time. Outside, they play with their family. They start eating a little grass and other adult foods, but they still drink their mother's milk. When they are five months old, the young prairie dogs will be fully grown.

Female prairie dogs stay with their families forever. Males leave home when they are two years old.

Be a
Prairie Dog Scientist

When a ferret is near a prairie dog town, the little animals need to find the closest burrow entrance and dive underground! Look at the picture and answer the questions.

1. Which hole should prairie dog A run to?

2. Which hole is closest to prairie dog B?

3. Should prairie dog C run to hole 3 or hole 4?

Use a ruler to measure between the prairie dogs and the holes. Were your guesses correct?

Glossary

burrow a hole or tunnel dug by an animal to live in

entrance a place to come in

females prairie dogs that can give birth to young

litter a group of baby animals born at the same time to the same mother

male a prairie dog that cannot give birth to young

mate to come together in order to have young

prairies large areas of flat land covered with grass

predators animals that hunt and eat other animals for food

territory the area where an animal lives and finds its food

warn tell others about danger

Index

Read More

Bodden, Valerie. *Prairie Dogs (Amazing Animals)*. Mankato, MN: Creative Education, 2023.

Nargi, Lela. *Grassland Biomes (Exploring Biomes)*. Minneapolis: Jump!, Inc., 2023.

Thomas, Rachael L. *Prairie Dogs: Builders on the Plains (Animal Eco Influencers)*. Minneapolis: ABDO Publishing, 2020.

Learn More Online

1. Go to **www.factsurfer.com** or scan the QR code below.
2. Enter "**Underground Prairie Dog**" into the search box.
3. Click on the cover of this book to see a list of websites.

About the Author

Rex Ruby lives in Minnesota with his family. He doesn't live underground, but he would love to explore a prairie dog's hideaway if he had the chance.